The
Busy People's
Bible Study Plan

THE
BUSY PEOPLE'S
BIBLE STUDY PLAN

Strategies for Personal Time with God
Amidst Life's Hectic Pace

Bertram L. Melbourne

Library of Congress Cataloging-in-Publication Data is available from the Library of Congress.

All Scripture taken either from the King James Version (KJV) or the *New King James Version* (NKJV).

Scripture marked NKJV taken from the *New King James Version*. Copyright © 1982 by Thomas Nelson, Inc. Used by permission. All rights reserved.

To modern Bereans
who will take time
to search the Scriptures to see whether
these things are so.

To my first students
in the course,
"How to Study the Bible and Enjoy It"
at Columbia Union College.

To all my teachers
who taught me how
to study and interpret the Word.

Contents

FOREWORD

We all remember Mark Twain's famous comment: "Everybody talks about the weather, but nobody does anything about it." We could update the saying for our day: "Everyone talks about the Bible, but nobody reads it." Dr. Bertram Melbourne wants to change that. He makes a great start in his new book *The Busy People Bible Study Plan: Strategies for Time with God Amidst Life's Hectic Pace*. Melbourne is talking to people in the real world. He is serious but not tedious. He makes the Bible user-friendly and approachable, and he takes the fear and mystery out of it. I have read the manuscript—now I want to get my hands on the book to share it with my family and friends. Melbourne has accomplished everything he set out to do. This is remarkable for a person who has spent most of his adult life in academia. I must say, however, that he did spend some time as a parish minister. This comes through when it gets to the application of what he is talking about.

Melbourne is a facilitator. I won't say he makes Bible study easy, but he does make it rewarding and even exciting. One thing he does well is to treat the reader as a responsible person, never talking down to us. This is not your usual how-to-do-it book. Immediately he challenges us to: "'Launch out into the deep and let down your nets for a catch' (Luke 5:4, NKJV). I invite you to leave the shallow areas and enter into the depths of faith and a deeper relationship with God" (pg. xii). Professor Melbourne would like to move us from being spectators to becoming participants. This approach will help us to interact with the biblical scene—its places, people, and situations.

He anticipates our excuses, our attempts to evade and postpone. The plan is for busy people. You must read how he and his wife and children used travel time to get their bible study in each morning. The plan is indeed workable—if—"there be a willing mind."

I find the various charts scattered throughout the book very helpful. Melbourne really brings it home when he deals with "Leading Questions to Get the Most from a Biblical Passage," which include: Who?

What? Where? When? Why? How? and Under what circumstances?
The suggestion that some readers may find it useful to keep a journal
of their bible study is appealing. You will find the section on tools for
effective bible study practical and useful.

Here is a little sneak peek into this important book as you prepare to
read it:

> Few of us have time even for the essentials in life—smelling the roses,
> relaxing with family and friends, spending time with God, etc. . . . Carl
> Jung says, 'Hurry is not of the devil, it is the devil'. . . People need to slow
> down to smell the roses and to develop lasting friendships with each other,
> but especially with God." (pg. 6)

Charles E. Bradford
President, Retired
North American Division of Seventh-day Adventists
10178 Sleepy Willow Ct.
Spring Hill, Fl 34608

INTRODUCTION

At the beginning of the last decade of the twentieth century, the chair of my department at the college where I taught invited me to teach a new course. The course, "How to Study the Bible and Enjoy It," was suggested on a fundamental principle that some think is flawed, others find objectionable, and yet still others consider factual. Some still do not understand why a course like that should be taught, and still others wonder why students should be encouraged to read and understand the Bible. At any rate, that was my assignment, and I gave it my best shot

I approached the course development with an open mind, desiring to be led by God to design a course that would capture the attention of young people living on the verge of a new millennium. Since the intent of the course was to help them develop a better appreciation for Scripture as the Word of God, this was of essence. I had a great experience in developing the course and preparing the material. Furthermore, teaching that very first class, with the 28 students who enrolled, was as memorable an adventure as all the subsequent repetitions of the course. Indeed, I gained insights that are not only invaluable for young adults but also for adults of all age groups.

Since I had always approached the task of teaching not just from the standpoint of an instructor but also from that of a learner, I came away from that assignment gaining a great deal of benefit. Insights on what I have learned, and my musings on them, are what you will find recorded in this volume for your consideration. I hope that you will find this work helpful and beneficial for your spiritual growth and development.

Why write a book on Bible study in an age when Bible study, even in Christian homes, is declining and in which the Bible, in the eyes of some, has lost its authority (see Lewy 1996, 75, 78). This excellent question deserves an equally good answer. Perhaps the issues that lie at the heart of such a question are what necessitate a book like this. Indeed, if the Bible is as old as it is claimed to be and if it can speak to contemporary issues, why shouldn't it be read? Read it as literature, if you wish; read it as history, if you so desire; read it for spiritual guidance, if you so choose, so long as you read it. It is my hope that the lasting value of this current volume will be the degree to which it stimulates others to read the Word of God.

One presupposition I take to this task involves the conclusion that many of us regard the Bible as the Word of God. It is also my belief that we would like to spend time reading it but, for one reason or another, find our schedules too busy for it. This book is intended to help you begin with what little time you can afford, use it to the maximum, derive maximal benefits, and be led to a deeper and more meaningful Bible study encounter. Hopefully, the final result will be a deepened, growing, and vibrant relationship with God.

Like Jesus, I say, "Launch out into the deep and let down your nets for a catch" (Luke 5:4, NKJV). I invite you to leave the shallow areas and enter into the depths of faith and a deeper relationship with God. Don't be satisfied with a mediocre association when you can have a deep, invigorating, satisfying, abiding, trustful, soul-satisfying one with this loving, benevolent, gracious, majestic, awe-inspiring, powerful, forgiving, and faithful heavenly parent. Why settle for an ordinary relationship with God when you can have an extraordinary one? *The Busy People's Bible Study Plan* can introduce you to such a relationship. Do you want it? Give it a try!

The Quiet Refreshing

Hush, hush, hush my soul!
This is not time to blush and fuss
There's no cause to push and shove
Its quiet time with One Who truly loves us

Now lay me down my cares
And set aside all my fears
'Tis time for me to dry my tears
For repose with One Who truly cares

Still, still with Thee in the morning
When my soul athirst is aching;
When human voice no calm can bring
And my heart and for you are breaking!

Hush, hush, hush, my soul!
Do you hear your Master speaking?
Bow down by His mighty footstool,
And listen to hear His quiet musing!

When every other voice and gadget is hushed,
And with a quiet attitude we bow before Him,
The silence of a soul thus humbled,
Is refreshed and blessed by peace from Him!

July 2008

Chapter 1

THE BIBLE AND CONTEMPORARY PERSONS

The Bible is the Word of God. It would be surprising to find many Christians who would reject the Bible outright. Besides, it is doubtful that the Devil himself would tempt us to do so. He knows he would not succeed. As a cunning and wily foe, he has found another and more effective way to trap us. He diligently works to make us neglect the Bible. In support of this notion, one could highlight the fact that while the Bible is the world's bestseller, it is a book with which many are still unfamiliar, especially those with education beyond high school (Lewy 1996, 78). Now, if we know the Bible is the Word of God, and if we know its value for success in daily Christian living, why would we neglect it? While only few people would intentionally neglect the Bible, I believe there are several unwitting contributing factors that result in neglect.

First, our contemporary culture contributes to the neglect of the Bible. Lewy calls our day "an age of secularism" (Lewy 1996, ix). It is a fast-paced, prepackaged, ready-to-consume, disposable, superficial generation. As such, many find it difficult, if not impossible, to dig deeply into anything. The primary question that is usually asked regarding anything seeking our attention or striving to make it into our busy schedules is: "What's in it for me?" Many people are disinterested in the Bible because they have asked this question and cannot find an adequate answer. Only items of high priority and great self-interest succeed in making it into our daily routine. But is this the best criterion to be used?

Moreover, it must be remembered that this is a postmodern society. For many, standards are not only questioned, but laws and Scriptures are seen as human constructs with no authoritative value. Besides, postmodern thought views God as a human way of explaining things that are otherwise inexplicable (see Liechty 1990, 5, 16, 37; Lewy 1996, x). What this means is that anything humans cannot explain, they attribute to what they call "God." God, then, has neither appeal nor authority, for "God" is a human creation. Surely, this kind of neglect inevitably leads to both rejection of God and the Word. Is it any wonder that the Bible has little or no appeal to many of our contemporaries?

Second, I also contend that what we bring to reading the Scripture will largely determine what we derive from it. How should we go to Scripture—as spectators or as participants? Apparently, we belong to a spectator generation. We sit beside the radio, in front of the television, or in the stadium/ballpark/arena to enjoy sports. Most of us are mere observers of sports activities; we are not actual participants. Many of us sit in front of the television or in the theatre to watch others perform for our entertainment. Because of this orientation, as well as our obsession with observation, some even go to church to watch people perform or to be entertained. We like to watch the choir sing and perform. We watch preachers read the Word, when they so choose. As a result, many of us do not read the Bible for ourselves anymore. This is a tragic development; as we said before, the benefits one derives from anything are usually commensurate to the time and effort invested.

Third, some of those who feast their mental appetites on novels and other fictional works are unable to appreciate Scripture due to its difference in genre. It is essential that I clarify this point. The point is that if the mind becomes addicted to a certain kind of literature, it will develop appreciation for that type to the exclusion of others. If this is the case, can there be any wonder that those for whom this notion has become a reality have great difficulty appreciating the Bible, since its drama and mystery are not as apparent? I found this to be true with my peers as we went through high school. Besides, my counseling has demonstrated it to be true of this generation of young people, as well.

A fourth factor involves a plan of the enemy to entrap us. We must constantly remind ourselves that we are in the midst of a cosmic struggle and that there are forces contending for our attention and the control of our minds. As such, the Devil has employed six minor allurements that he has made major distractions in our lives and experiences. He uses them to divert our attention from important issues and to preoccupy our minds with trivia. Note them below. I am indebted to Richard Foster and his *Celebration of Discipline* for the first four (1998, 15).

1. Busyness

Some of us are so busy that we end up being too busy for God. But what does Bible study have to do with busyness? Perhaps more than we think. In order to sustain an appreciable lifestyle and make ends meet in this high-tech, fast-paced, space-age, text-messaging, podcasting generation, many of us have become very busy. Whether we have to work two jobs, or have to keep up with our children's programs, or are occupied with church work, many of us are extremely busy. We get so busy that there is not enough time for Bible study or communion with God.

How much time do you spend each day with the Bible? A comparison with the time spent daily with television, video games, and the Internet could be instructive. A 1999 survey reported that the average American child spent 25 hours per week watching television, 7 hours playing video games, and 4 hours using the Internet (http://www.media.family.org/research/report_mqexecsum.shtml). A 2005 study is also informative. It noted that the average American 8- to 18-year-old spends an average of 4 hours and 15 minutes daily watching "Screen Media" (this includes TV, DVDs, handhelds); 49 minutes playing video games; 1 hour and 2 minutes using the computer (see http://www.kff.org/entmedia/upload/Generation-M-Media-in-the-Lives-of-8-18-Year-olds-Report-Section-4.pdf); 50 minutes on homework; 43 minutes reading; 25 minutes watching movies; and 2 hours and 17 minutes hanging out with parents in hobbies, or physical or some other kind of activity (http://www.kff.org/entmedia/entmedia030905nr.cfm?RenderForPrint=1). Note the time children spend weekly with each activity in the chart below:

TV	Playing Videos	Internet	Home-work	Non-school Reading	One-on-one with Parents	Father	Mother
25 hrs	7 hrs	4 hrs	4 hrs	0.5 hrs	minimal	0.5 hrs	2.5 hrs

It has been determined that "by the time the average American reaches age 65, he or she will have watched about nine entire years of television— the equivalent of watching 78,000 episodes of *Survivor*," a conservative number estimated by the TV-Turnoff Network (see http://www.tvturnoff .org/images/action/AmLivedocsrpt.pdf).

In a 2005 study that labeled the current generation of young people Generation M, the *M* standing for "media," the Kaiser Family Foundation found some very revealing data on the use of the media by 8- to 18-year-olds. It was discovered that they spend an average of 6 hours and 21 minutes a day with media. When broken down this represents an average of "4 hours watching TV, videos, and DVDs; about 1.75 hours listening to the radio or CDs, tapes, or MP3 players; slightly more than 1 hour a day on the computer outside of schoolwork; 49 minutes a day playing video games; and 43 minutes a day spent reading books, magazines, or newspapers for something other than schoolwork." The study also found that the time spent with media far superseded that spent with parents (2 hours and 17 minutes), hanging out with peers (2 hours and 16 minutes), engaging in physical activity (1 hour and 25 minutes), pursuing hobbies or other activities, and doing homework (50 minutes) (http:// jbpub.com/samples/076374154X/Page_Emotional%20Well-Being_4e _Ch03.pdf).

Merton Strommen found that most church homes rarely discuss God, the Bible, or matters of faith. Eight thousand youth from Protestant or Roman Catholic homes were asked how often they gathered as a family to discuss God, the Bible, or some religious issue. Forty-four percent said it never happens, 32 percent said it happens approximately once a month, 13 percent said once a week, and 10 percent said daily (Strommen 1998, 9). Where does your home fall? Is it represented in this survey? What would your children say?

Sample Size	Frequency	Percentage
8,000	Never happens	44%
	Once monthly	32%
	Once weekly	13%
	Daily	10%
	Unsure	1%

There are those who suppose that attendance at a Christian college, membership in a church, tenure of office in a religious organization, or participation in some social project can substitute for quality time with the Word of God. But not only are they mistaken, they are misguided. Busyness is more than of the Devil; it is the Devil's favorite tool and is designed to keep us distracted.

The point is: people make time for that which is important to them. As such, if study of the Word is important to us, we will make time for it. How else can we explain the statistics on the time spent with television in comparison with the Word of God? While many Christian youth no longer can tell Bible stories or recite verses from memory, it's nothing for them to narrate the plots of many soap operas, recite the names of many movie stars, or repeat the lyrics of many songs. It has been documented that movies, television, video games, and the Internet have done a lot to condition the thinking and appreciation of today's youth. Consequently, they have no regard for that which is not packaged in the same format as these productions. Thus, these things capture their imagination, and the Word of God is neglected. Something must be done to reverse this trend.

2. Crowds

Some people have great difficulty with being alone. We have an insatiable desire to be with others. We need the crowd. It is true that God made us gregarious, fond of company. But we must watch our dependence on the crowd, for it is fickle and must not be followed blindly. Besides, we should remember that the same crowd that on Sunday morning sang, "Hosanna! Blessed is He who comes in the name of the LORD!" (Mark 11:9; cf. John 12:1, 12–15) shouted "Crucify Him! . . . Crucify Him!" on Friday (Mark 15:13–14; cf. Matt. 27:20–25). This seems to be the result of what is called "mob psychology." Interestingly, the Hebrew Scriptures had cautioned against following a multitude to do evil (see Ex. 23:2). It would behoove us to heed that warning.

3. Noise

Silence is boring for some of our contemporaries. They need the radio, television, DVDs, MP3 players, cell phones, the Internet, or PDAs for companionship. But God bids us, at times, to be still and know that He is God (Ps. 46:10). One author says, "When every other voice is hushed and in quietness we wait before him, the silence of the soul makes more distinct the voice of God" (White 1905, 58). There is a Spanish proverb that is germane. It says, "*el silencio es oro.*" Its translation is "silence is golden." Perhaps, to beat the enemy, we need to practice it!

4. Hurry

Contemporary people, especially in certain large cities, are always on the move. We are always hurrying to go here or there. This might not all be negative, but the result is still the same. Few of us have time even for the essentials in life—smelling the roses, relaxing with family and friends, spending time with God, and so forth. Carl Jung says, "Hurry is not of the Devil, it is the Devil" (Foster 1998, 15). People need to slow down to smell the roses and to develop lasting friendships with each other, but especially with God. But how can this be if we are too busy for communion with Him through His Word—the Bible? One lesson from September 11, 2001, is that, while we still have the opportunity to do so, we all need to take time to communicate our true feelings to those who are dear to us whether or not it is considered macho. Most importantly, this includes our true feelings of love and appreciation toward God.

5. Worry

Many people tend to spend valuable time worrying about problems. Worry is a tool of the Devil designed to distract us. While the Lord invites us to cast all our cares upon Him since He cares for us, worry places the focus on our attempts and ourselves at independence for problem solving. The fact is, selfishness and independence were at the root of the original sin and are still at the root of all sin. Besides, I have never known worry to solve any problem. Instead, it causes problems to escalate. I invite you to stop worrying and accept the invitation of Jesus to cast your problems on Him. Do you have the faith to prove Him to see if He will come through for you?

This is a trust factor, and worry strikes at its very heart. This is why the wise man admonishes us to "trust in the LORD with all [our hearts] and lean not on [our] own understanding" (Prov. 3:5, NKJV). The Devil specializes in getting us to believe it is difficult to lean on the Lord, but we need to prove him a liar. So vital is this point that the Bible, in at least 69 places, admonishes us to trust in the Lord. The Prophet Isaiah even promises, "You will keep him in perfect peace, Whose mind is stayed on You; Because he trusts in You" (Isa. 26:3, NKJV).

6. Things

The enemy keeps us preoccupied with acquiring and using things that distract us from the essentials in life. To keep up with the proverbial Joneses is the life goal of some of our contemporaries. People have become so engrossed with things that their values have become skewed. We are called upon to love people and use things. However, in our society today, too many people love things and use people. This is the Devil's trap. We must re-evaluate our priorities and resist the Devil's temptations.

I, therefore, encourage believers not to allow distractions to keep us away from the Word of God. We need to recognize the lies of the Devil for what they are. We need to ensure that we put first things first in our lives. Again, I believe that the Bible can be understood by all, is relevant to contemporary individuals, and can be employed in the solution of life's problems. Perhaps the most important issues are the why and how of Bible study. Or, again, how can this ancient Book be made relevant to those living at the dawn of the third millennium?

Happiness Is…

Happiness is more than a feeling;
It is a way of life guaranteed
Happiness is more than just believing.
It is the fruit of a soul regenerated!

Happiness is not just a feeling
Generated by the acquisition of toys;
Happiness is a quality of living
Motivated by practicing eternal joys!

Happiness is not a destination to seek
It's not just a place about which we preach
Happiness, my friend, is an attitude we keep
It's a mode of travel for which we daily reach.

Happiness is not found in things material,
It is more than attaining the good life;
Money or riches can't buy this gift eternal,
Found in an enthusiastic attitude to life.

So then, let's be up and doing
Not feeling, toys or things pursuing
But, an attitude of daily life adopting
Guaranteed by His Word daily reading!

Updated from author's original
July 2008

Chapter 2

WHY SHOULD THE
BIBLE BE STUDIED?

W e have seen that the Bible is the Word of God, that it can edify contemporary persons, and that it can assist in resolving modern issues. It now remains for us to consider the reasons why it should be studied. At issue are crucial questions such as: What is in Bible study for me? What will I get from its study, and what will I miss by not spending time with the Word of God? Is there lasting value in the study of the Word that should cause me to interrupt my daily routine to insert a new detail? These are valid issues. There are several reasons why the Bible should be studied.

1. The Bible contains hidden treasure.

People today are preoccupied with becoming wealthy. There are so many game shows specializing in helping people to become millionaires or to win large sums of money. Some people, who can't make it onto these shows, spend their last dollars on lottery tickets in the hope of winning the jackpot. Yet, many have unused wealth at their fingertips. In one of His parables Jesus said, "Again, the kingdom of heaven is like unto treasure hidden in a field, which a man found and hid; and for joy over it he goes and sells all that he has and buys that field" (Matthew 13:44, NKJV).

What kind of treasure is to be found in the Bible? I suggest eternal ones. The Bible tells how eternal life was achieved and how it can be obtained. The author of the first gospel reminds us that it was through Jesus' sacrifice of Himself that eternal life was achieved and that we obtain it through faith (John 3:16). If indeed this life with its problems will be destroyed and if in fact there is a way out, should we not want to discover the way?

A legend tells the story of a father who died telling his sons that there was a treasure buried in a field. They spent their time digging up the field to discover the treasure. Unfortunately, they found none and wondered why their father had played such a trick on them. One brother came up with the brilliant idea that since the field was already plowed, they should plant crops in it. The abundant harvest revealed to them that the treasure was not hidden gold, but the potential for abundant yield in the agricultural use of the field.

The Bible is such a gold mine—neglected, yet full of treasure. It is a fertile field to be taken seriously, for it is ripe for exploration to extract its treasures. But, it will take time, effort, commitment, and dedication for its exploration. The rewards are invaluable, and it yields fruits not only for time but also for eternity.

A mother gave a youth a Bible when he was leaving home. He kept the Bible but did not use it. Years later, when faced with depression and discouraging circumstances, he decided to give the Book a try. He was shocked at the relief it brought. In fact, it changed his circumstances and turned his life around. Later, he expressed shock that he had allowed himself to suffer so much while he had neglected such a helpful tool right there in his very possession.

2. The Bible is a Word of God to us.

The prophets contend that the Word of God came to them (see Isa. 2:1; Jer. 1:4; 2:1; Ezek. 1:3). They are communicating that they claim no rights to their words. Though recorded in their own words, they imply that God is the authority behind what they wrote. As such, what they wrote can be regarded as the Word of God to His people. Peter concurs with this notion, observing, "And so we have the prophetic word confirmed, which you do well to heed as a light that shines in a dark place, until the day dawns and the morning star rises in your hearts . . . for prophecy never came by the will of man, but holy men of God spoke as they were moved by the Holy Spirit" (2 Pet. 1:19–21, NKJV).

If the words are from God, then we must listen. We must listen to the voice of our Creator. It is against this background, therefore, that we should understand the psalmist's declaration: "How sweet are Your words to my taste, sweeter than honey to my mouth!" (Ps. 119:103, NKJV). And again: "Through Your [words] I get understanding" (v. 104, NKJV). If the psalmist is correct, and we believe he is, then the Bible must be studied as the Word of God to humankind for our comprehension.

3. The Bible must be studied because it contains truths and principles that are essential to successful living.

The Bible answers life's crucial questions: Who am I? Where did I come from? Where am I going? In other words, it gives us knowledge. The Bible gives us knowledge in the following areas:

Origin—Genesis 1:1, 26–27; 2:7; Isaiah 1:3; Romans 3:23

These texts suggest we are creatures. They speak of our Creator and the act by which He made us. The prophet Isaiah goes a bit further when he proposed that the ass knows its owner and the ox its master's crib; yet, Israel does not consider (Isa. 1:3). Isn't this a strong indictment? Don't we, therefore, need to know our origin? There's only one place where this can be found—the Word of God. It must be taken seriously and must be used for its designed purpose.

Reason for being—Matthew 6:19–21; Ecclesiastes 12:13; Philippians 2:15; 1 Peter 2:9

These passages suggest that the purpose of our being is to fear God, give Him glory, develop character, and adopt the mind of Christ. We need to do this because we are a people of God's own choosing, designed to show forth His praises (1 Pet. 2:9). Moreover, if we are a people separated from our Creator by sin, why are we here? What is the purpose of our being? What does God expect of us? These questions must be answered, and the Bible has the answers. We cannot therefore afford to neglect the Word of God. We are obligated to use it.

Destiny—Ecclesiastes 12:13–14; Romans 14:10–12; John 3:16; 5:25–29

Here we are reminded that there is an impending judgment in which all of us are obligated to appear to give account of how we have lived our lives. God sent His own Son to die to give us the best destiny there could ever be—eternal life—but we must desire it, and we must choose it. He has set before us two choices, and we are accountable for the one we make. These destinies are recorded in the Word, and the rewards and punishments associated with each are outlined there also. The wise person will therefore want to become acquainted with them; that is why people will want to spend quality time with the Word of God to become familiar with these destinies and the mind of God.

Do you need this kind of information? If the answer is yes, then you need to study the Bible. I need it, and that is why I value the Word of God and make time for its study.

4. The Bible is a good guide.

The Bible is not only a good guide; it is that and more. It is the best guide. The psalmist says, "Thy word is a lamp unto my feet and a light unto my path" (Ps. 119:105, KJV). It is the best guide and can illuminate pathways because of its heavenly connections. "Thy word" implies that it is the Word of God. It is this connection with a divine source that gives meaning, authenticity, and validity to the Bible. This divine connection makes the Bible the best guide. It can therefore be the pilot to guide those who are preparing for a destiny with God. That is what the psalmist counsels regarding its efficacy in Psalm 119:9–11, 17–19.

Furthermore, we are admonished to study God's Word if we are serious about salvation and if we want to show ourselves approved of God as workers who can rightly understand the Word of truth. Why would one want to understand the Word of truth? So that it can lead to God, since it is the greatest guide that one can have in this world to point the way back to a relationship to God, a relationship that was lost through sin.

I have met many young people through the years who were drifting aimlessly through life. However, when they came in contact with God's Word and yielded to its transforming influence, their lives changed and took on new significance and meaning. I recall the experience of one young man in particular. When he came in contact with the Bible, it had such an impact on him that he gave up a life of drugs and was transformed into a preacher of righteousness. His first task today is the proclamation of that transforming Word to see if it can be as efficacious for others.

5. The Bible supplies the spiritual needs of the mind and the will.

Our minds need the influence of the Word of God each day. We are bombarded continuously by information and influences that are not conducive to Christian living. The effect of our materialistic and secularized society on the minds of Christians is extremely negative. Thus, there is need for a counteracting force to save our thinking pattern and sustain its Christian character. This is what Bible study is designed to do (see Ps. 119:11). If we are Christians who are committed to Christ and who want to maintain our status as such, then daily Bible study is imperative. We need it to help fortify our minds against the negative influences of a secular and humanized society.

Many of us can truthfully testify that what has made the difference in our lives and what has kept us through the vicissitudes of life has been the influence of God's Word. It has made the difference in my life when I faced discouraging circumstances and problems. On one occasion, when it seemed I would be overwhelmed, I opened my Bible. Imagine the reassurance I found when my eyes fell on the words: "Fear not, for I am with you; Be not dismayed, for I am your God. I will strengthen you, Yes, I will help you, I will uphold you with My righteous right hand" (Isa. 41:10, NKJV). The Bible can provide that same kind of help for you, too, if you give it a chance. Will you allow it to have that influence in your life?

6. Bible study is a valuable preventative medicine and an antidote against sin.

The psalmist once observed: "Your word I have hidden in my heart, That I might not sin against You" (Ps. 119:11, NKJV). Do you hate sin? Do you hate it enough to want to get rid of it? If you do, then why don't you treasure the Word of God and hide it in your heart so it can act as God's great antidote against sin in your life? The Bible is the written word that gives us information about the living Word—Jesus Christ. It says He hated sin so much that he resisted unto blood fighting against it (Heb. 12:1–4). Sin cannot reside where He abides; so if we treasure the Word in our hearts and allow it to lead us to a living and abiding relationship with Him, then we can have lasting protection against the Devil and sin.

A youth once found himself in a compromising situation. He went out with the wrong crowd and was about to do what was wrong. He was now sorry, but it appeared to be too late. He could see no way out of his dilemma. He knew what he was about to do would grieve his parents. He knew it was wrong, but the influence of peer pressure was strong. In anguish, he cried to God for help. As he struggled, the words of a scripture immediately popped into his mind. It said: "My son, if sinners entice you, Do not consent" (Prov. 1:10). It gave him the courage to stand for what he knew to be the right thing.

7. The Bible reveals Christ and His love for us.

The Bible is the Book that tells us of a God who loves us so much that He gave His only Son to die on our behalf. Furthermore, it tells us of a Savior whose love for us motivated Him to die on our behalf when we were His enemies (see John 3:16 and Rom. 5:8). No other book has a comparable answer to the sin problem. No other book tells of a God who is so intimately identified with His people.

The Bible is not only a theological treatise with which religious scholars wrestle, but it is also a practical lesson guide for the average Christian. I knew a man who could not read but had a fervent desire to do so. One day as he walked along the street, he saw a few pages from the Bible lying around. He picked them up and fervently asked God to help him read them. A miracle occurred in his life. From that day on, for the rest of his life, the only book he could read was the Bible. We who can read need to add Bible reading to our reading enjoyment. You, too, can begin habitual and enjoyable Bible study. Why don't you vow to continue your communion with God through His Word? I invite you to pledge to make communion with God your habitual practice.

The Book Divine

Holy Bible! Book divine!
Precious treasure, thou art mine!
Mine to tell me whence I came;
Mine to teach me what I am;
Mine to chide me when I rove;
Mine to show a Savior's love;
Mine to guide my wayward feet;

Mine to judge, condemn, acquit;
Mine to comfort in distress,
If the Holy Spirit bless;
Mine to show by living faith
Man can triumph over death;
Mine to tell of joys to come,
In the saints' eternal home;
O thou Holy Book divine,
Precious treasure, thou art mine!

                              —John Burton

Life by Measurements

By the nail, life goes like a snail;
By the mil, it can go a long mile;
By the inch, life certainly isn't a cinch;
By the foot, it may take a long loop;
By the yard, life can be very, hard;
By the rod, it may require a long nod.
By the centimeter, life requires a center;
By the liter, it requires a good leader;
By the furlong, life can go real wrong;
By the mile, life could be very mild;
By the league, life may have much fatigue;
But by the **Word**, it not only has light;
Life becomes explosive as dynamite,
Takes on the splendor of the divine,
And inches all the way to the father's house.

Updated from author's original
July 2008

Chapter 3

PREREQUISITES FOR ENJOYABLE BIBLE STUDY

I s it really possible to enjoy Bible study? How can this Book, whose most recent pages date back almost 2,000 years, be really owned by modern people? Further, how can a Book, the oldest portions of which go back more than 3,500 years, still be relevant in this age? Do you really believe that a Book written in and for an agrarian society can speak to the needs of people in this high-tech, space-age, Internet-using, gene-cloning generation that is standing on the threshold of the third millennium?

We have suggested that it can, for it is universal in its scope and unlimited in its appeal. The Word of God has an attraction for all peoples in all generations. It is, therefore, valuable to the lives of contemporary humankind. Given these truths, how then should its study be approached? What should a person in this modern society do in order to derive maximum benefit from the study of this ancient document? Are there necessary prerequisites to enjoyable, meaningful, and effective Bible study?

You bet there are! Just as there are predetermined criteria for entry into certain organizations and stipulations for association with certain groups, so there are conditions to be met in order to gain maximum results from time spent with God's Word. It is a law of life that one does not get more from anything than the time and energy one is willing to invest in it. If we value the benefits that can be derived from God's Word and from association with Him, then we'll make time to spend with Him, for there would be no sacrifice too great to make for this kind of fellowship. Here are some suggested prerequisites for beneficial and enjoyable Bible study:

1. Accept the Bible for what it is—the Word of God.

Treat the Bible reverently and read it prayerfully. It is God's communication of Himself and His ideals for His people. Stand in awe before it, but not just for its sake as much as for the authority of the One who is behind it—the Supreme Creator and Sustainer of the universe.

2. Approach Bible study with an open mind and a willingness to learn.

Don't go to Bible study with a closed mind and fixed opinions. Instead, approach the Bible with a mind open for the Spirit to teach you what your divine guide deems best for your growth and development. Expressed another way, God would like to fill some of us with blessings, but we cannot be filled. We must be emptied of pompous attitudes, bigoted opinions, superficial ideas, or pseudoscientific notions. If we must study to be approved of God, we need open minds that are willing to learn the many things the Spirit has to teach us so that we may bring the goodness of God into our lives.

3. Approach Bible study with a willingness to hear the voice of God.

Since the Bible is the Word of God and since we are to approach it with open minds, it stands to reason that if we approach it in that spirit, we can learn a great deal from it. This learning is contingent upon our willingness to stop to listen and hear the voice of God. But which of us should not want to listen to our Creator, especially when He invites us to call to Him and He will answer (Jer. 33:3)? Let that one stand up, and I will show you one who neither knows his origin nor his destiny. When the Creator speaks, His creatures should listen. Since Scripture is one way in which God speaks to us, then we must stand in awe and listen.

4. Go to Bible study understanding that the Bible was written for people of a time frame, culture, language, and geographic area different from ours, to address their needs and problems.

It is a theological axiom that one must first discover what a text meant for the original readers before determining what it means for us today. This fact must neither be ignored nor taken lightly. Two illustrations might illuminate this point. First, when I was growing up, if I said to my friends, "I feel gay today," they would have understood that I meant I was happy. If I should dare utter those same words today, they would carry a totally different connotation. Upon hearing them, some would wonder if I were coming out of the closet. If such a dramatic change in word meaning could have occurred in my brief lifetime, think of the changes that could have occurred over the last 2,000 years with respect to the New Testament. not to mention the last 3,500 years when the Old Testament is considered.

Second, 1 Thessalonians 4:15 in the King James Version states: "we which are alive and remain unto the coming of the Lord shall not prevent them which are asleep." What does this mean? How can the living saints prevent those that are asleep? Does it mean we will not prevent them from going to heaven? This is the implication in today's understanding of the word *prevent*. However, when the King James Version of the Bible was translated into English in 1611, *prevent* meant "to precede." The implication was that the living saints would not precede those who died to the glories of heaven.

When Paul wrote that passage in the first century, he was saying there would be the same glory for those who die and those who remain. Thus, those who are alive to see the Second Coming would not get to heaven before, or have any advantage over, those who died. Yet, the passage of time and changing meaning of words could have caused confusion. Again, this illustrates why it is important to discover what a text meant in order to find out how it applies to our contemporary situation.

5. Commit yourself to spend quality time with God on a daily basis.

Getting the most out of Bible study does not come from a onetime stand or haphazard time with Scripture. On the contrary, quality time must be committed to this task. If indeed God's mercies are new to us every morning and His faithfulness is great, as Jeremiah contends in Lamentations (3:22–23), why can't we at least commit to studying His Word daily? Why can't Christians have the same commitment to the Word of God that sports fans have to sports or those who watch soap operas have for their shows? Really, my position is that there should be greater commitment. But, given the lack of it, I would settle for equal commitment, at least.

6. Approach Bible study with humility.

The ultimate author of Scripture is the Creator. We must have reverence, awe, and respect for His Word. The Bible records the experiences of humankind with the Creator, but it is more than just that. The Bible is divine self-disclosure for the benefit and education of His creatures (see 2 Tim. 3:16–17; 2 Pet. 1:21). It is God's revelation of Himself to us. We must, therefore, humble ourselves before it.

7. Vow to spend some time each day in solitude with God, listening to His voice as He speaks to you.

God still speaks to His people, and He wants to speak to you, too. You must make time for Him. Time must be made when the distractions of this fast-paced, high-tech society are put away and shut out. Develop a quiet place for silence and solitude so that you may see and hear the Word. Time devoted entirely to and exclusively for communion with God brings equilibrium to our lives and stability to our schedules.

8. Commit yourself to keeping a spiritual journal.

The value of this exercise is found in your ability to record your thoughts and God's communications with you. There are invaluable insights you will gain in your study. Left unrecorded, they will be lost forever. However, if they are kept in a private journal, then they could provide blessings for you in later times of discouragement or in low spiritual moments. The practice of keeping a journal allows you to ponder the meaning of what is studied and to hear God speak to you in a new way through your study as you write. The point is that, if recorded, your spiritual insights will always be available to provide spiritual edification for you or your loved ones.

9. Commit yourself "every day and for the rest of your life" to make your most important choice be your relationship with God.

This is your most important task in life, for your most vital association is in your relationship with a God who has loved you so much that He sacrificed Himself for you on a tree. Is this too great a commitment to make for One who loves you so much? Someone I know once had the following sign in two prominent places in his office:

> *My most important appointment each day is my appointment with God.*

Could this prescription assist you in daily living? Why not adopt it and implement it through daily Bible study?

Enriching the Days of Our Lives

> As we walk each day these halls we call life,
> May we strive a passion for integrity to acquire!
> May we seek like Him to make a difference!
> And touch some heart with the rays divine.
>
> May it be our goal to spend each day caringly,
> Warming a heart; nurturing a mind and cheering a soul;
> May each of us spend our days on this earth wisely,
> Doing, caring, loving, and living our lives for the King.
>
> Yet to attain this, an attitude to life we must acquire
> Which, my friends, in ordinary books we'll never find.
> It's found only in daily communion with the Father
> Through thoughtful study of His Holy Book divine!
>
> I invite you to commit to daily study of this timeless book
> Its abundant blessings won't only be in this life terrestrial
> Open the book; take a look; so it can become a hook,
> To enrich your days on this sod, and lead to life celestial

July 2008

Chapter 4

BIBLE STUDY AND YOU

I recently read that the average person will waste enough time in 10 years to earn a Ph.D. degree from any university. This suggests that we all waste some time each day. Is it true for you? How can we better utilize some of this time? How can we make more productive use of our spare time? What if some of this time was spent in productive Bible study? We are all busy people, but how much of this time would you like to commit to spending with the study of the Word? Keep in mind that we all make time in our schedules for those things that are important to us. Is communion with God through His Word important to you? Then make time in your daily routine for it.

It is also true that many of us approach Bible study from the wrong perspective. Consequently, we do not derive as much blessing as we could or should. When I was growing up and I was introduced to Bible reading, the objective was either to read the Bible through in one year or to memorize as many texts as I could. I was certainly blessed, and it helped to improve my memory. Notwithstanding, I now know that I could have derived more if I had employed another approach to my study, even if I had not accomplished the task of reading the Bible through. Moreover, I was not taught to apply what I read to my life and to contemporary life situations.

It is within this framework, therefore, that I presume to suggest a way to a more productive study of the Bible. It is called *The Busy People's Bible Study Plan* (BPBSP). I do not assume that it will fit the needs of every Bible reader. It may not. Besides, others may find problems with it just as I had problems with that on which I was raised. This is just another suggested method of Bible study that can be employed to assist in cementing and giving a foundation to the spiritual lives of some people.

The essence of this method is its emphasis on the utilization of minimum time for maximum benefits. To achieve this goal, the primary focus is placed neither on the length of the passage read nor on completion of the Bible in any specified period of time. The focal point of this method concerns quality accomplishments, not quantity results. We suggest that a small passage of Scripture be selected. It is preferable that the passage selected contains no more than five verses. These verses should be read and reread under the guidance of the Holy Spirit until they possess you and until the Spirit interprets them to your heart and mind.

As you read, place yourself in the situation described and feel with the characters. Additionally, there are some leading questions that you should keep foremost in your mind, seeking answers to derive the maximum benefit from your time with the Word of God. These questions are not exhaustive. They are a beginning. Use them to start and then develop other questions of your own. Remember also that whatever method of Bible study you use, it is not an end in itself. It is only a means to an end. It is designed to lead you into a better understanding of the Word and a deeper relationship with God. It is my hope that as you read and put into practice the principles of the BPBSP, you will develop a more meaningful relationship with God.

"But what are these leading questions you mentioned? Aren't you going to share them with us? I most certainly will! They are the focus of the next chapter. Let's go!

What Is Time

Time has been variously defined,
And many, many answers given
By different folks refined;
And those by whom it's driven.

How do you define time, my friend?
Do you describe or do you define it?
What is time to you, my friend?
The sound of a clock going tick, tick!

Certainly time is more than that;
It is a gift given us by a loving God
Use wisely doing more than just chat
For, we must account for its use on this sod.

The word of God surely tells us about time,
It invites us to redeem the time we have
For the day are evil and full of crime;
So to time, let's never ever be come a slave!

Time is made up of seconds, minutes and hours
It's much too precious to be idled away;
Spend it wisely, my friends, for it is ours
And it will be gone forever some day!

Time for me is a long interlude in eternity
Carved out by God for us sinful humanity;
To develop characters fit for life in eternity;
And show we're ready to live with divinity.

July 2008

Chapter 5

Leading Questions to Get the Most from a Biblical Passage

To take you quickly into the heart of a passage and to help you understand the main issues and recognize the important characters, I suggest the following questions. Again, please note that they are not exclusive, nor are they the only questions. They are questions that I have found most helpful and that have been extremely helpful to others, too. Therefore, I am recommending them to you.

First, to determine the major characters in the passage as well as the place of its occurrence, you must ask the following series of questions: *Who? What? When? Where? Why? How?* Seek answers to these questions as you read. It should be noted that sometimes all the answers to these questions might not be present in a given passage. However, you should ask them anyway because it is only when you do that you'll discover which are indeed answered. Also, note that the answers may not be in the sequence given and sometimes all the answers may not be located in one sentence or in one verse.

Second, what is the central thought of this passage? What is its primary focus, and how does it fit in with the overall scheme of the chapter and/or book? What does the passage say about God or about Jesus Christ?

Third, how do you feel about what you have read? Ask yourself the following questions:

- *How do I feel emotionally?* To gain the maximum benefit, you must enter into the passage and not just stand as an outsider observing what is taking place. Participate in the passage. Consider yourself as one of the characters and feel with that character as you proceed—see the sights, hear the sounds, smell the aromas, taste the food and drink, and touch the people and things. Yes, use your imagination. It can be very helpful in understanding Scripture.
- *How do I feel spiritually?* Is the message of the passage applicable to my life? Will it make me a better person? Is the behavior displayed one that I can adopt or is it one I must avoid for successful Christian living? Seek honest answers and do not be superficial in your quest.
- *How does this passage apply to my life, my own situation, and me?*
- *What is God communicating to me through this passage?* Be willing to listen, because communication is not a one-way event. It is a two-way channel.
- *Is there a thought in this passage to guide my life today?*
- *Is there a promise to claim?*
- *Is there a thought to share today?*

Before proceeding further, let us explore how this works by applying it to a passage or two. Let's apply these questions to Romans 12:1–2 (translation mine) to see what we might learn from this passage. It reads:

> I urge you therefore brothers and sisters by the mercies of God to present your bodies to God as living sacrifices, holy, well-pleasing, the kind He will accept, which is the only rational thing to do and is an act of spiritual worship. Stop assimilating yourself to the manner of living of this age, but continue to be metamorphosed by the renewing of your mind so that you can prove what God's will is—His good and well-pleasing and perfect will.

1. Who?

There are several "whos" in this passage. Let us consider two. The first one is "I." Who is this "I?" To determine this we must go back to the beginning of the book. The most obvious inference is that it refers to the author of the book of Romans, whom we know is Paul. The second one is "you." To whom does the "you" refer? Again, we must return to the first chapter of the book where we will determine that the "you" must refer to the recipients of the book, whom we know to be the Christians in Rome.

However, we know that it would also refer to readers of the first century and all subsequent readers.

2. What?

There are at least two "whats" in this passage. The first is "Beseech you . . . that you present your bodies a living sacrifice . . . to God." The second is "Stop assimilating yourself to the manner of living of this age, but continue to be metamorphosed" (paraphrased).

3. When?

The "therefore" suggests that the appeal is made the basis of the argument advanced thus far. If that is true—and it is—then on the basis of Romans 3:21 and 8:1, among other texts, we have to conclude that this must be done **NOW**.

4. Where?

Christians may present themselves wherever they wish.

5. Why?

It is the only rational thing to do in view of all Christ has provided for us in justification by faith, and it is an act of spiritual worship.

6. How?

There are at least three "hows": "by the mercies of God"; "holy and well-pleasing"; and "by the renewing of your mind."

7. What is the central thought of this passage?

The central thought seems to be an appeal for Christians to present themselves as sacrificial love offerings to God, instead of continuing to let the world dictate their manner of living.

8. What does it say about God or Jesus Christ?

It is through the mercies of God that believers are able to make acceptable sacrificial offerings to God. Besides, even that laudable act is not achieved through human effort. It is God's doing through His abundant grace. Furthermore, by implication we could also deduce that because of the sacrificial death of Jesus on the cross, we do not need to present either dead animal sacrifices or our dead selves as a sacrifice to God. Jesus paid it all.

9. How does this passage apply to my life, my own situation, and me?

The appeal is for me, (insert your own name), to present myself to God in a healthy and fit condition. This means I must eat right, exercise daily, and abstain from all harmful drugs and intoxicants, as this is an act of spiritual worship for me. It also means I must stop allowing the world to motivate or dictate my manner of living. Finally, it means I must continue to allow my mind to be transformed so that my thinking is consistent with God's will for my life. In that way, I can prove that God's plan for my life is best.

- *Is there a thought to guide my life?* God needs me alive with all my energies in His service to do His bidding. Furthermore, my giving myself to Him is an act of spiritual worship, which is the only rational thing to do in view of what was done for me in Christ.
- *How do I feel about what I have read?* I must respond positively to this appeal. It is for my betterment.
- *How do I feel emotionally?* I love God. I thank Him for the salvation He has provided in Jesus. Is there anything too hard for me to do for such a God? No! Love begets love. I can do what is required as my love offering to God.
- *How do I feel spiritually?* I feel it is my spiritual duty to respond to this appeal by giving my all. Apart from God, I am nothing. It is He who makes me something and someone. It is, therefore, not only my spiritual duty; it is my loving response.
- *What is God communicating to me through this passage?* He is saying that my gift of myself to Him must be as acceptable and spotlessly

pure as the sacrifices Israel offered in the Old Testament had to be. This is not a call to perfectionism, but rather a call to total commitment to God through sacrificial living.

- *Is there a thought to guide my life today?* God has a plan for my life, and it is best for me, because He is the Creator and He designed it especially for me. A loving response to God is the only rational response, and it is an act of spiritual worship.
- *Is there a promise to claim?* God's promise is to help me present myself as an acceptable offering to Him.
- *Is there a thought to share today?* God loves you, and, because of the demonstration of His love for you, you should love Him, too, as well as His other children in our midst.

Again, I do not presume these are the only responses to these questions. As the Holy Spirit guides you in your personal study, you might derive others. These responses are only intended to demonstrate what is possible. It is plausible that if I should begin again, I might even come up with other answers. The point is that there are no right or wrong answers. As you seek God's guidance and yield yourself to the Spirit's leading, there is no limit to what He can and will accomplish in and through you.

Now, it might be helpful if you would choose your own passage and apply this methodology to it and seek what you can derive from it. Some folks might ask where they should begin. This is a good question, but it is hard to legislate. Where to begin differs according to individual needs. A good starting point for some could be the Gospels. One prolific writer on biblical themes concurs with this notion and recommends that we spend a thoughtful hour each day in contemplation on the life of Christ (White 1940, 83). However, here are some other helpful suggestions.

The Bible has great biographies. Some readers who love biographies could begin with the life of their favorite biblical hero, such as: Moses, David, Esther, Joseph, Daniel, or Miriam. Intriguing and interesting histories can also be found in the pages of the Bible. Readers who love history could begin with a passage from Genesis, Exodus, Deuteronomy, Samuel, Kings, Chronicles, Acts, or elsewhere. Some readers love geography. They will find interesting reading material in the geographical descriptions found in such places as: Exodus, Deuteronomy, Joshua, Ezekiel, Luke, Acts, Revelation, and so on. Those readers who love literature can begin with the poetry of the Psalms or with Job, Ecclesiastes, Proverbs,

Song of Solomon, Lamentations, or 1 Corinthians 13. Romance stories are also found in Scripture, so those who love to read romance can go to Song of Solomon; or the story of Isaac and Rebecca; or Jacob, Rachel, and Leah; or to the book of Ruth. The following chart gives an idea of some of the categories of material contained in the Bible and where they can be located.

Type of Material	Some Examples
1. Literature	
a. Autobiography	Galatians 1:11–2:10; 2 Timothy 4:5–8
b. Biography	Genesis; 12: 1–25; 21:1–26:35; 25:19–50:26; Ruth; 1 Samuel; Luke; Matthew
c. Poetry	Job; Psalms; Proverbs; Lamentations; 1 Corinthians 13
d. Romance	Genesis 12–30; Ruth 2–4; Song of Solomon
e. Wisdom Literature	Ecclesiastes
2. History	Genesis; Joshua; Judges; Samuel; Kings, Chronicles; Acts
3. Science	Job

If you are not interested in a thematic approach but want to begin with passages, here are a few suggestions that are already delimited for you:

Mark 6:6–8	Hebrews 12:1–4	Luke 5:1–11
Ephesians 1:15–20	John 3:16	John 14:1–3
1 Peter 1:1–5	Hebrews 11:23-27	Romans 8:1–3
Philemon 7–9	Philippians 2:5–11	Romans 6:1–6
Philippians 3:7–11	Philippians 4:8	Micah 6:7–8

The point is that where you begin is entirely up to you. It is best for you to begin where you are most comfortable and where the Lord directs you to begin. In the final analysis, it does not matter where you begin. What we are most interested in is that you begin somewhere and that you begin an adventure with God that can last a lifetime. Indulge yourself and see how you fare. I promise you that you will never regret it. Perhaps your only regret, if any, will be to discover that you waited too long to start. Will you begin today?

Don't Hurry or Worry; Be Blessed

People in life are always in a hurry,
Going hither and yon some task to perform in a flurry
But Karl Jung says hurry is not of the devil but the devil
Slow down; take time for the essentials of life, like a smile.

People in life always love to worry;
And so live their lives in sorrow
All because they love to borrow
From the perceived ills of tomorrow

I therefore invite you my dear friends
To stop and take time to smell the roses;
Stop living life at the behest of these fiends
Make time for a God who truly cares!

Accept the call found in His Word
To cast your every care upon Him
Not only does He care but He's the Lord
Who created you and the seraphim!

So, make time for Him in your life
Spend time with Him and be blessed
For with Him life is never stiff
But will end in eternal bliss!

July 2008

Chapter 6

THE STRUCTURE OF
THE BUSY PEOPLE'S BIBLE STUDY
PLAN

The essence of the BPBSP is its flexibility. It can be adapted to the time constraints of those who use it. It aims at allowing users to design Bible study to fit the time input that best suits their needs and that is affordable. Its goal is to provide maximum benefits from crunched time commitments. As such, one can adapt it for use whether one has 10 minutes or 60 minutes.

When utilizing this method, therefore, the first task one has is to determine how much time one can afford to realistically spend in Bible study. I cannot give you one time that will fit all. What I would suggest is that you select the time that best suits you. For the purpose of illustrating the BPBSP, I will use two times—20 and 30 minutes.

The second task has to do with selecting your passage for study. Determine this before you begin. I would suggest that a few verses—five or six at the most, preferably three—be selected. Make sure the passage you choose is a unit. This means you should ensure that all the verses selected are dealing with the same thought or idea. For example, while Romans 12:1–2 is about the justified Christian's relationship to God, verse 3 deals with a new thought—the Christian's view of self; and verse 4 onward treats the social and interpersonal relations of Christians. Verses 1–2 would therefore form a unit, as would verse 3, though verses 4 and 5 could possibly be taken with verse 3 without too much difficulty. The same is not true of verse 6. It definitely goes with what follows it.

With these preliminary matters out of the way, you are now ready to embark on a discussion of how to utilize the chosen 30 minutes for maximum benefit. Be sure to adopt what follows to the available time you have in your personal schedule.

How do you gain the maximum benefit from 20 to 30 minutes of Bible study? Just as several tasks are involved in preparation for Bible study, even so there are steps involved in the process of Bible study itself. Thus, the time must be divided among these tasks. Please note carefully that the focus is not so much on the time spent on each step as on the steps themselves. As such, two models are presented. The first has no time limits while the second has. The point is that some of us love structure while others hate it. What I have tried to do is configure the BPBSP to accommodate both needs.

Again, I must warn you that the time is presented as a guide. It is not intended that you sit with a stopwatch by your side slavishly following the time limit. What is intended is that you divide your time among the various tasks to allow you to gain maximum benefit. If it seems artificial at first, just keep on doing it until it becomes a part of you. Keep in mind the old adage "Practice makes perfect." The following table outlines the program and gives a comparison of the two approaches. Choose the one that best suits your style of learning and/or study habit. Note also that the model that outlines the time element also allows choice, since it outlines activities for both 20 and 30 minutes.

Activity	Model One Time spent in activity	Model Two Time spent in activity
Step 1—Solitude	A couple minutes	1–2 minutes
Step 2—Prayer for God's guidance	A few minutes	1–2 minutes
Step 3—Read and reread the passage	Most of the time	8–10 minutes
Step 4—Silent reflection	A few minutes	3–5 minutes
Step 5—Record your thoughts in a journal	Some time	5–7 minutes
Step 6—Thanksgiving	Remaining time	2–4 minutes

A New Year's Plea

Before you O Lord, today we come,
At the start of another New Year.
More like you, we want to become,
Give us power our trials to bear.

Grant us vision your Spirit to seek,
Give us valor his biddings to follow;
Grant us courage your will to keep;
For only thus will we daily grow!

This new year as an open book,
Lies straight ahead for you and me,
In twelve months how will it look?
Will it still be bright and new?

Come into my heart now Lord Jesus
For closeness to you we daily strive,
Come Holy Spirit reside always in us
For your guidance we need to thrive.

Updated from author's original
July 2008

Chapter 7

THE PROGRAM

When you have chosen the model from the last chapter that best suits your needs, use the time outlined for each activity to accomplish the tasks listed in the left-hand column and the following outline.

Step One: Spend time in solitude to recognize the presence of God.

At the burning bush, Yahweh told Moses to remove his shoes from off his feet, since His presence made the ground where Moses stood holy (Ex. 3:5). The children of Israel had to wash themselves and their clothes in preparation for entrance into God's presence (see Ex. 19:10–11). The sons of Korah spoke to Israel on God's behalf in song, saying: "Be still, and know that I *am* God: I will be exalted among the nations, I will be exalted in the earth!" (Ps. 46:10). Now, if Israel had to show deference for the presence of God, why shouldn't we?

What is being argued here, therefore, is for Bible readers to take time out from their regular activities to prepare for entering into the presence of God. This does not mean they have to go take a bath or wash their clothes. This suggests that they need to take time to change the focus from themselves and their daily routine to concentrate on preparation for entrance into the presence of a Holy God. We are sinners, and He cannot behold evil. Thankfully, Jesus is our advocate and, through Him, we gain access to God, the Father. However, we need time out for transitioning from mundane activities to stand in His presence.

Now, this is not necessarily a time for prayer. Yet, if you find yourself praying, do not worry about it. That is great. This is a time-out for a pause designed to help us acknowledge entrance into the presence of majesty and to help us leave behind anything that annoys or bothers. It is time to be used to shut out all distractions and prepare for communion with God. No radios, MP3 players, or televisions should be used, even if equipped with religious music or programming. This is just time for you and God alone—yes, you alone with God. Remember the words of Ellen White: "When every other voice is hushed and in quietness we wait before Him, the silence of the soul makes more distinct the voice of God" (White 1905, 58). This time is your chance to make the most of one-on-one communion with your Creator.

Note carefully that this is time to change the focus of your attention from the mundane to the heavenly. It is designed to help you place your entire focus on your relationship with the divine.

Step Two: Use some time to pray for God's guidance and the illuminating power of the Holy Spirit as you read the selected passage.

Again, this is not a general prayer or a time designed to ask God for things you desire or want. No, it is prayer to seek God's guidance as you read His Word so you can gain maximum benefit from what you read. Perhaps you should pray after you have read the passage through once. Then you can be specific about the ideas you need help to adequately comprehend. You can also pray for God to bring to your attention those things He deems most vital for your personal, spiritual, Christian growth and development. Your ideas of your need might be totally off-center, but His ideas should be right on. He knows us more than we know ourselves. He is our manufacturer, and He ought to know what is best for us. We need to cease from making demands and requests and begin to listen to His suggestions and recommendations.

Step Three: Devote most of the time to reading and rereading the passage to get into its essence or central thought.

Sometimes I am asked whether the Bible is only for scholars who have the tools and theological expertise to unravel its deep, hidden truths. I emphatically submit that it is not, as this process will show. Yes, the scholar can dig deeply into the Word, but under the illumination of the Spirit the nonscholar can also derive great benefit.

I well remember an assignment given by the late Dr. Edward Heppenstall in a class I took from him. He invited each of us to select one of several difficult passages from the Bible and unravel its meaning without the use of any biblical tools or aids. My passage was Colossians 2:13–17. For me, that was a life-changing assignment. As I grappled with the text, I read it and reread it. I used several modern translations and, finally, after much digging and the guidance of the Holy Spirit, I was able to get into the text and comprehend it. My job was so thoroughly done and the Spirit's assistance so complete that, when Dr. Heppenstall read my paper, the good doctor was sure I had had outside help and asked for my bibliography. I had to remind him that he had asked us not to use study aids. That could be your experience, too.

I am, therefore, recommending that you read and reread the passage. Use as many translations as you wish and be sure to compare and contrast them, noting the similarities and the differences, so that you can get at what the passage is saying.

As you read, seek answers to as many questions of the Bible study method, as possible, that we have highlighted thus far. Write down your answers in a notebook. You will need them later.

Step Four: Now use some time for silent reflection.

After you have gone through these exercises, you need to spend some time in silent reflection. You have read, and you now need to think about what you have read and the implications for your life, your relationship with God, and your interpersonal relationships. During this time, listen to the Holy Spirit speaking to you. Concentrate on what you have read and its applications. React to what you have read and draw conclusions.

Apply your findings to your life. Seek a promise from the passage that could bring cheer to your life. Seek also a thought by which to live or a truth to share.

We should read the Bible for more than mere coverage; we should read it reflectively to be inspired by its great truths. Read to benefit your personal development but also read with an idea to share the Gospel with someone. Just as Jesus took time to share life with you, and the Holy Spirit took time to illumine your mind, read with a view to derive some benefit that can be shared with someone else. Read personally, reflectively, and relationally.

Step Five: Now record your thoughts and reflections in your journal.

Your journal need not be a commercial one that has ideally formatted journal sheets and preselected passages. Use that kind if you so choose, but remember that that may take away your individuality from the passages you want to select. My recommendation is that you choose any hardcover notebook that you specify for that purpose. Moreover, in these days of cell phones, MP3 players, PDAs, laptops, and so on, your journal need not be in book form. The outlined steps can be followed on any of these devices with which you are comfortable. What you need to do is to write the date at the top of each page as well as the passage you are reading; then you can proceed to record your thoughts.

Remember this is your own personal, private journal in which you are recording your personal thoughts for yourself. Therefore, be free to be yourself and to express yourself. Outline your doubts, your fears, your questions, your frustrations, your joys, and so forth. Record the thoughts you find to guide your life. Write down the thoughts you find to share. Write out whatever you think will be of benefit to you or a thought you would not want to forget.

Step Six: Use the remaining time to thank God for His guidance and illumination.

This is a prayer of thanksgiving and praise. Use it as such. At times you can write out your prayers in your journal as well. Some people find it easier to write out their prayers. There is nothing wrong with this practice.

Try it if you are comfortable with it. If not, leave it alone. What you do in your Bible study and prayer time is entirely up to you and is your choice. It cannot and must not be legislated by anyone else. Be creative. Be thorough. Be spontaneous. Be guided by the Spirit, and be true to yourself and your God.

Hope for the Days of Our Lives

O God who alone gave stability in ages past,
And who alone is our hope for years to come;
We look to you always with hope steadfast
Assured you identify for man you did become.

We seek you claiming your charge to:
Not let our hearts be troubled or be afraid;
We come clinging to your promise that:
You'll one day take us to dwell with you.

We come to you knowing you are resurrection and life,
We come with hope of a better land and a brighter day;
We come hoping for that land where there'll be no strife
Yes Lord, we come with anticipation of that fadeless day.

While we now sorrow because of life in a world of pain,
We despair not as those who only have hope in this life
We long for a new day when goodness will forever reign
When sin will be vanquished and there will be no strife.

Thank you for making such great plans for us,
Thank you for always planning for our best good;
Thank you for your word you sent to enlighten us,
And serve as guide for our feet in every likelihood.

Until then, take us your hurting children in your care,
Nurture us thru refreshing encounters with your Word;
Keep us looking to You for strength to live without fear,
Sustain us thru a daily infilling of your spiritual sword.

Grant us a faith that will withstand,
The tribulations of trying days ahead;
Help to always trust your guiding hand
Even when we do not fully understand!

We long for a land where there'll be no more tear;
We long for a day when fear will be known no more;
We long for a time when tears are dried never to reappear;
We long for that glorious day that will last forever more.

(Continued on next page)

So be to us the Good Shepherd who his sheep will not betray,
Prepare green pastures in which we may each day reside;
Guide us through the bad times and the good with Thy ray
Restore our souls and give us a faith that will long abide.

Updated from author's original
July 2008

Chapter 8

ALTERNATE APPROACHES

P erhaps some of you might be too busy to find the time for 20 or 30 minutes to read the Bible in one sitting. I have thought about your situation and will make provision for you, too. Included in this chapter are suggestive plans that could meet your needs, too.

Plan One

A few years ago my wife and I were at a gathering of friends. We chatted for a while, and now I don't recall the subjects. What I do recall, though, is that one friend began sharing with the rest about what we had taught him about Bible study. Since we were clueless about what he referred to, my wife and I looked at each other. Imagine our chagrin when he recalled how his family had spent some time with us a few years earlier and were impressed with how we had morning devotions.

You see, when my children were small, we had only one automobile. My wife had to get to work at 7:30 a.m., I had an 8:00 a.m. class, and we had children in two or three different schools. To get all the children ready, prepare and eat breakfast, as well as beat the rush-hour traffic to get to work on time, we had to have our morning devotion in the car as we drove along. While I drove, we all sang, my wife read the Scriptures, the children asked questions, we all interacted, and they took time to pray. We had a wonderful time of bonding and fellowshipping with each other in a car five days a week for more than a year. We enjoyed it and took it for granted, but it was impressive to others. It is this kind of creative Bible study that I now recommend to you.

Perhaps you have several automobiles in the home, as we do now, so the experience above might not be convenient. However, what about getting the Bible on CD, DVD, PDA, iPod or cell phone? What about spending some time meditating on God? What about playing some music that could set the mood for reflection? How about then playing and replaying a few verses of the Bible either from your CD, DVD, PDA, or cell phone and meditating on them?

You could then reflect on the Word and, when you have some appropriate time, record your thoughts in a journal. Could this not be a good way for busy people to enjoy Bible study instead of not having any Bible study at all?

If your travel time to work is 45 or 50 minutes, why not try the following?

- Devote five minutes listening to meditative background music during which you could enjoy thoughtful meditation in preparation for entrance into the divine presence.
- Devote a minute or two to invite the Lord to guide your mind and thoughts as you listen to His words. Seek His illumination as you listen to His Word and His guidance as you travel in traffic.
- Devote 15 minutes to listen and re-listen to a selected portion of Scripture. Listen to it until you get into its thoughts and understand what God is saying to you through it.
- Spend three or so minutes reflecting on what you have just heard. Ask the Holy Spirit to help you apply it to your life, and seek specific areas that could be improved or enhanced by what you have heard.
- Spend a few more minutes recording your reaction to what you have read. It is also possible to do a journal on your computer or PDA. If you prefer a written journal, write out your thoughts later.

Plan Two

I have used another method of Bible study that could be helpful for busy people in the new millennium. At times, I go walking in the early morning on a track at a school close to my home. Since I have the Bible on CD, I take a CD player with me and listen to the Word as I walk. Isn't that something you, too, could do?

If you go jogging or walking in the outdoors or if you work out at a gym or in your own basement, why not add Bible listening to your routine? Perhaps you could spend a minute or two in thoughtful meditation and reflection as you enter the divine presence. You could then seek God's guidance as you listen to His Word. Ask God to illumine your mind and to flood your thoughts with ideas and insights that are applicable just for you and your life.

Now choose a book of the Bible to begin listening to on your CD, DVD, PDA, iPod, or cell phone. Devote as much time as you need to listening and re-listening to a few verses as you walk, jog, or work out. As with reading, the objective is not coverage as much as it is deriving benefit from what is read. We suggest that you read for depth of understanding.

When you are through listening, you could then use a recording device to record your thoughts and reactions to what you have read. This step is very essential, for it helps you to keep a record of your thoughts and reactions. In this way, you could have your own ideas and reflections to benefit you in times of stress and discouragement. Why must you always be paying for other people's thoughts when you could be benefiting from your own too? Remember that God has blessed you with insights and understandings that can be vital if you would just take time to write them down or record them for future use. God blesses you just as much as He blesses others. Furthermore, if the authors of the books we read did not take time to record their God-inspired thoughts, we would not have had those books to read. I am, therefore, inviting you to record your thoughts and insights from your Bible study.

Plan Three

There is a third alternative for those who have the Bible on their computers or PDAs. You could select your passage and read it on your device, then follow the steps as previously outlined. These gadgets grant you the opportunity to copy and paste so you can select your passage, paste it on your page, and write your heart away. Both your prayers and thoughts can be written out. Besides, they grant the opportunity to do Bible study with the aid of modern technology.

Walking the Walk and Talking the Talk

I walk the way of the cross,
I talk the talk of Christ;
I shun the way of the loss
I long for home with Christ.

The talk of Christ, I talk
The talk of the world I shun;
At the world's deeds I balk
Least in me its work be begun.

I talk the talk of Christ
I run the Christian race;
I walk the way of Christ
I shun ways not of grace.

The Christ of the cross I love
He describes it for me in His Word;
The entrance of which bringeth love
To bless those traveling heavenward.

The way of the cross I love
The way of the cross I'll walk
The way of the cross leads home
So I'll take it all the way home.

July 2008

Chapter 9

HELPFUL TOOLS FOR ENJOYABLE BIBLE STUDY

As you begin to enjoy Bible study, there are some tools that you will find valuable to your understanding of the Word. These tools can assist word studies or can serve to give background information on the geography, culture, peoples, customs, or flora of the biblical world. I will also suggest a few commentaries that you might find helpful. I will arrange these tools in categories so that you can have a variety from which to choose.

A Good Bible Dictionary

Choose from the following:

Achtemeier, Paul J., gen. ed. 1985. *Harper's Bible Dictionary*. New York: Harper Collins.

Douglas, J. D., ed. 1979. *The New Bible Dictionary*. Grand Rapids, Mich.: William B. Eerdmans Publishing Company.

Freedman, Noel D., gen. ed. 1992. *The Anchor Bible Dictionary*. 6 vols. New York: Doubleday.

Horn, Siegfried. 1981. *The Seventh-day Adventist Bible Dictionary*. Rev. ed. Washington, D.C.: Review and Herald Publishing Association.

Marshall, I. H., A. R. Millard, et al. 1996. *New Bible Dictionary*. 3rd ed. Downers Grove, Ill.: InterVarsity Press.

Maynard, Jill. 1997. *Reader's Digest Illustrated Dictionary of Bible Life and Times*. New York: The Reader's Digest Association.

- You should note that the *Holman Bible Dictionary* is also available online or on CD-ROM through Parsons Technology.

A Good Bible Commentary

Begin with a good one-volume commentary, such as the following:

Church, Leslie F., ed. 1975. *Commentary on the Whole Bible by Matthew Henry*. New one volume ed. Grand Rapids, Mich.: William B. Eerdmans Publishing Company.

Jamieson, Robert, et al. n.d. *A Commentary: Critical and Explanatory on the Old and New Testament*. Grand Rapids, Mich.: William B. Eerdmans Publishing Company.

Richards, Lawrence O. 1987. *The Teacher's Commentary*. Colorado Springs, Colo.: Chariot Victor Publishing.

- You should also note that several commentaries are also available online or on CD-ROM through Parsons Technology or Logos Software, including the following:

  The New Commentary on the Whole Bible
  The Bible Knowledge Commentary
  The Teacher's Commentary
  Matthew Henry's Commentary

A Good Book on Bible Manners and Customs

Choose from the following:

Freeman, James M., and Harold Chadwick, eds. 1998. *The New Manners and Customs of the Bible*. Plainfield, N.J.: Bridge-Logos Publishers.

Gower, Ralph. 1987. *The New Manners and Customs of Bible Times*. Chicago: Moody Press.

Vos, Howard F. 1999. *Nelson's New Illustrated Bible Manners and Customs: How the People of the Bible Really Lived*. Nashville, Tenn.: Thomas Nelson Publishers.

A Good Concordance of the Bible

Choose from the following:

Cruden, Alexander. 1954. *Cruden's Unabridged Concordance*. Westwood, N.J.: Fleming Revell Company.

Strong, J. n.d. *The Exhaustive Concordance of the Bible*. McLean, Va.: McDonald Publishing Company.

Young, Robert. 1951. *Analytical Concordance to the Bible*. Grand Rapids, Mich.: William B. Eerdmans Publishing Company.

- Additionally, the *New American Standard Exhaustive Concordance* is available online and on CD-ROM through Parsons Technology.

A Good Bible Encyclopedia

Choose from the following:

Bromiley, Geoffrey, ed. 1994–95. *The International Standard Bible Encyclopedia*. 4 vols. Grand Rapids, Mich.: William B. Eerdmans Publishing Company.

Drane, John William. 1998. *Nelson's Illustrated Encyclopedia of the Bible*. Nashville, Tenn.: Thomas Nelson Publishers.

Packer, J. I., M. C. Tenney, and W. White Jr., eds. 1995. *Nelson's Illustrated Encyclopedia of Bible Facts*. Nashville, Tenn.: Thomas Nelson Publishers.

A Good Handbook of the Bible

The following are examples of some that are available:

Alexander, George M. 1962. *The Handbook of Biblical Personalities*. New York: Seabury Press.

Alexander, Pat, and David Alexander, eds. 1999. *Zondervan Handbook to the Bible*. Grand Rapids, Mich.: Zondervan Bible Publishers.

Gugliotto, Lee J. 1995. *Handbook for Bible Study: A Guide to Understanding, Teaching, and Preaching the Word*. Hagerstown, Md.: Review and Herald Publishing Association.

Pilch, John J., and Bruce J. Malina, eds. 1993. *Handbook of Biblical Social Values*. Peabody, Mass.: Hendrickson Publishers.

Unger, Merril G. 1998. *The New Unger's Bible Handbook*. Chicago: Moody Press.

- Additionally, the *Holman Bible Dictionary* is available online or on CD-ROM through Parsons Technology.

A Good Study Bible

There are many from which to choose, especially the modern speech versions. A few are listed here. African Americans would do well to choose from one of those specially designed for them like *The Original African Heritage Study Bible* or *The African American Jubilee Edition*.

The American Bible Society. 1999. *The Holy Bible: The African American Jubilee Edition*. King James Version. New York: ABS.

Barker, Kenneth, gen. ed. 1985. *The NIV Study Bible: New International Version*. Grand Rapids, Mich.: Zondervan Bible Publishers.

Felder, Cain Hope, gen. ed. 1993. *The Original African Heritage Study Bible, King James Version*. Nashville, Tenn.: The James C. Winston Publishing Company.

Robertson, A. T. 1931. *Word pictures in the New Testament*. 6 vols. Nashville: Broadman Press.

Suggs, M. Jack, Katharine Doob Sakenfeld, and James R. Mueller, eds. 1992. *The Oxford Study Bible*. Revised English Bible with the Apocrypha. New York: Oxford University Press.

The Life Application Study Bible. 1997. Grand Rapids, Mich.: Tyndale/Zondervan Bible Publishers.

The NIV Full Life Study Bible. 2004. Grand Rapids, Mich.: Zondervan Bible Publishers.

The NIV Knowing Jesus Bible. 1999. Grand Rapids, Mich.: Zondervan Bible Publishers.

The NIV Men's Devotional Bible. 1993. Nashville, Tenn.: Zondervan Bible Publishers.

The NKJV Nelson Study Bible. 2005. Nashville, Tenn.: Thomas Nelson Publishers.

The NKJV Woman's Study Bible. 2007. Nashville, Tenn.: Thomas Nelson Publishers.

The NKJV Word in Life Study Bible. 2003. Nashville, Tenn.: Thomas Nelson Publishers.

Freedom's Song

I cried, I wailed, I wept, and I bawled.
God of our ancestors, if you are there, where are you?
O God, I cried, I wailed, I wept and I bawled
I'm sad, I'm tired, and I'm angry at You.

I hear about torture, I hear groans, I hear whips.
I see misery, I see inhumanity, I see a chain.
I see torture, I see wounds, I see rape and I see ships.
I touch a corpse. Where is my brother? I feel pain!
O God where are you? What is there to gain?

O God, where am I and do you really care?
I'm out there in the middle some where and I feel caged,
They tell me that your Good Book says that you do care?
I'm in the middle of a passage where all I can do is stare.
I'm tired, I'm angry, I wail, I stare. Do you really care?

Hush! Hush! There seems to be music somewhere;
Yes, there is music everywhere, someone says;
Songs of anticipation, songs of freedom fill the air,
O God, do You care, as Your good Book says?

I feel like a piece of firewood in a heap,
I'm so cramped, that I can't sleep;
And this singing really numbs the pain,
And so for the moment there is some gain.

Look! I see a new land.
Maybe here there will be a new plan
For Lord knows I can't stand—
The sights and sounds of the old plan!

But alas! The suffering gets worse,
I thought there was a brand new plan;
Yet I see masters and whips with a new dose
Of pain and suffering in this new land.

God of my ancestors, where are you? Do you care?
I have cried, I have bawled, and I have dared
To struggle; read your Book, and sing in my little cage
Oh yes, I'm waiting for You to show me that You care.

O my Lord, I hear singing in the air,
Just as you Good Book said would happen;
Oh yes I anticipate jubilation with great flair
For with singing we will gladden the heaven.

Not too long thereafter, the bells did ring,
Not too long thereafter, the people indeed did sing,
And peeling out were songs of freedom and redemption,
Oh my God, is there finally a way out of this situation?

Then God whispered, O dear child!
I was in the dungeons of humiliation with you;
I was in the boats of the Middle Passage stacked up beside you;
Without me, the heat and cold, the sun and rain would have devoured you!
O yes, I was there; hearing and answering your prayers and soothing you!

Some things are hard to understand, my child;
The Book say in me at all times you must trust
For no evil deed goes unpunished, my child;
And, "joy comes in the morning" to the just.

So you descendants of the African Diaspora,
For the cause of justice and freedom I have freed you;
So, never enslave anyone and never be a slave to another,
For, it was for the cause of freedom and justice I freed you.

You'll find this in the Book I have gave you
To guide your weary feet on the long way
Leading to the place I'm preparing for you;
Use it as your map and read it as you pray.

So, shout for joy you children and ring the bells of freedom;
Celebrate the results of what once seemed impossible;
Ring dem bells, sing dem songs and dance dem dance of freedom
And let's celebrate the achievement of the improbable.

Peoples of the African Diaspora, let freedom ring!
Ring it out! Let them hear what the Book tells you!
Shout with joy and let no one again enslave you,
By God's grace never again let freedom escape you!

July 2008

Chapter 10

CONCLUSION

T hanks for spending time with me in these pages. I appreciate your reading it. Now that you've read it, don't just put it down, as you might do with other books. I invite you to do something with and about the information you have gathered from it. Tell someone else about it. Encourage them to reflect along these lines. Most importantly, I urge you to put these principles into practice in your own life and experience.

I invite you to begin a relationship with God through the BPBSP. By now I hope it is has led you into a deeper thirst for God. From what you have read, I believe you can find a new plan for a new millennium. If you begin by spending 20 or 25 minutes with the plan each day, I guarantee you that as God begins to bless you, as you begin to enjoy the fruits of spending quality time with Him, you will extend that time and make your relationship with God your most important task each day. While Guenter Lewy sees a "crisis of unbelief" in this "age of secularism," and while Richard Foster views superficiality as the curse of our age (see Lewy 1996, ix; Foster 1998, 1), continued use of the BPBSP will lead you beyond the shallows of superficial Bible reading into the depths of a new and deeper relationship with God. Indeed it will lead you into a new relationship that is befitting to a new millennium.

I challenge you therefore in the words of Luke 5:4 (KJV) to "launch out into the deep" for a new and deeper relationship with God. Take time to pray, ponder, and study every day. Do it when you feel like it and when you don't feel like it. Make it a habit that you cultivate. It will bear fruit through time and into eternity. Don't let anyone or anything rob you of that deep, abiding association with God that comes through spending time alone with Him each day.

Happy adventure! And as you enjoy it, introduce others to the program so that they can enjoy it, too.

Busyness

Too busy to study the word of God
Some wisecrack once told me
What he really meant was too busy for God
The One who gave His best for you and me!

Too busy for God is the cry of a world gone mad
Young and old, short and tall and rich or poor
Have all now embraced this new, new fad
And thus their Maker and do now abhor!

But this too was predicted in the Word of God
That said in the end perilous times would come
For men would love pleasure more than God
Now it appears those days have certainly come.

Too busy for my God I could never become
Especially when I think for me what He's done;
No one else would leave heaven and come
To earth to die even if I was the only one.

Too busy of God, how silly can mortals be!
For their Creator, Sustainer and Redeemer is He
The Great One who thru His power let them be
No such silliness for me; What about thee?

Busyness is the hallmark of our age that's evil,
But do you know what Karl Jung once said?
Busyness is not of the devil; it's indeed the devil
And believe me that is truly, truly, truly sad!

July 2008

SELECTED BIBLIOGRAPHY

Foster, Richard J. 1998. *Celebration of Discipline: The Path to Spiritual Growth*. 20th anniversary edition. New York: HarperCollins.

Henry J. Kaiser Family Foundation. 2002. Key facts. Menlo Park, Calif., and Washington, D.C., http://www.kff.org/entmedia/loader.cfm?url=/commonspot/security/getfile.cfm&PageID=14092.

Lewy, Guenter. 1996. *Why America Needs Religion: Secular Modernity and Its Discontents*. Grand Rapids, Mich.: William B. Eerdmans Publishing Company.

Liechty, Daniel. 1990. *Theology in Postliberal Perspective*. Philadelphia: Trinity Press International.

Strommen, Merton P. 1988. "Why Business as Usual Is no Longer Possible." Draft presentation on societal trends to a planning conference, January 5, 1988, at Loma Linda University, Calif.

Strommen, Merton P., and A. Irene Strommen. 1985. *Five Cries of Parents: Help For Families on Troublesome Issues*. New York: HarperCollins Publishers.

TV-Turnoff Network. *Real Vision*. Washington D.C. http://www.tvturnoff.org.

TV-Turnoff Network. SCREENED IN: How Excessive Screen Time Promotes Obesity. http://www.tvturnoff.org/images/action/AmLivedocsrpt.pdf.

White, Ellen G. 1905. *The Ministry of Healing*. Mountain View, Calif.: Pacific Press Publishing Association.

————. 1940. *The Desire of Ages*. Mountain View, Calif.: Pacific Press Publishing Association.

Thank You Lord for Your Word

Thank you for your Word dear Lord,
Telling us of your great love for us,
Of your Spirit who dwells inward
And tells of your Son's death to save us.

Thank you for you Word dear Lord,
It's a lamp to our feet to guide us,
Light for the path going heavenward
A map on the road right to keep us
Like tonic it gives strength for the road.

Thank you for your word dear God,
It's like sugar, it sweetens our life
It's like oil and floats above any odd
Like an instrument it brings music to life!

Thank you for your word, dear God,
It's defensive gear like a bullet proof vest;
It's an offensive weapon like the sword;
It's protective covering that beats any test;
It offers the best protection at home or abroad.

Thank you God for being true to your Word
When you gave your Son to die to rescue us
Thank you dear, dear Lord just for being You
A giving, loving, and forgiving friend for us!

July 2008

Afterword

In this book, as the title says, Dr. Bertram Melbourne unites two features of our modern culture that need to be explored together—busyness and inadequate study and/or reading of the Bible. It is true that our generation is consumed by busyness. Melbourne shows that not only is this a fact to be noted, but it is also not one to gloat about in light of Karl Jung's observation that "busyness is not of the devil but is the devil."

Melbourne shows that the consumerism and spectator-oriented nature of our age when coupled with busyness make for a bad combination—the neglect of key aspects of life including smelling the roses and studying God's Word. Using research laid out in charts, Melbourne demonstrates that our contemporary generation does not spend much time reading or studying the Bible. He then shows that busyness contributes to the lack of time spent with the Bible, and therefore one needs to look at the choices one makes in regards to lifestyle and time management in order to spend ample time with the Word.

To assist readers in making these choices, Melbourne gives prerequisites for enjoyable Bible study. He notes the value one can derive from its study. What is interesting here is the statement he presents about the amount of time people waste. It is quite revealing that the average person wastes enough time in ten years to earn a Ph.D. from any university. He is correct that we all make time for those things that are important to us, so if study of God's Word is important to us we will make time for it. He gives the reader leading questions—who, what, when, where, etc.—to ask a biblical text so as to get the most out of his or her Bible study. I found the section listing the types of material found in the Bible—such as poetry, history, and biography—valuable. He not only lists the type of material, but he gives examples of each for the benefit of the reader.

Yet, these preliminary steps are just the building blocks to take the reader to the "real stuff," which is the structure of the *Busy People's Bible Study Plan*. The essence of Melbourne's Bible plan is flexibility. Two diverse models are presented—one using about twenty minutes and the other utilizing approximately thirty minutes. Though somewhat demanding, the plan as presented, especially with respect to journaling, does allow busy people to spend just twenty or thirty minutes and have a rewarding time with Bible study.

The emphasis on quality time with the Word rather than quantity coverage is refreshing. So too are Melbourne's attempts to have people reflect on and pray about what they read. The call to journaling means this will not be a one-time or easily-forgotten effort. Rather, things chronicled in the journal will be available for future reflection and refreshing to the reader. The tools for deeper study that are given in the final section of this book are very helpful to the reader for use in his or her future study. Yet, how will busy people find time to use these resources? It appears Melbourne hopes to have his readers hooked, so that after completing their reading and implementation of his ideas, they will want a deeper look at the Word which will ultimately result in Bible study becoming a way of life.

In the sample passages and themes presented, I feel included as a woman. I see attempts at balance in the presentation of the material. In sum, I enjoyed reading this work, and I recommend it. I think it is valuable for the church and Christians.

Dr Barbara Williams-Skinner

President, Skinner Leadership Institute

Founder, Congressional Black Caucus Prayer Breakfast